Bub Escapes from the Reptile!

By Sally Cowan

Sim and Bub sit in the sunshine.

Bub sips from some rosebuds.

Meanwhile, Sim naps.

Hey Dad, are you awake?
Can we have a flying contest?

OK! Let's dash to the grapevine and back!

But before they can dash off,
they see a big shape!

It sideswipes the rosebuds!

Sim and Bub can see
a very, **very** big reptile!

It seems very hostile!

Sim and Bub do a steep nosedive to hide in some pinecones!

Pim glides onto the pinecones.

Did you see that reptile flag
on the flagpole?
It is so lifelike!

“Dad, we made a silly mistake!”
said Bub.
“That reptile is not alive!”

Excuse me, Bub!
I was not very brave!

Sim and Bub have their
flying contest.

They dash to the grapevine,
around the flagpole
and back again!

"You amaze me, Bub!" said Sim.

“But can you beat **me**, Bub?”
said Pim.
“Female birds are very quick!”

“Let’s go!” said Bub.

CHECKING FOR MEANING

1. Where did Sim want to race with Bub at the start of the story? *(Literal)*
2. Where did Bub and Sim end up racing? *(Literal)*
3. How was Bub feeling at the end of the story? *(Inferential)*
4. Was Sim and Bub's racing route a good one? Where else could they have raced? *(Evaluative)*

EXTENDING VOCABULARY

grapevine	What are the two smaller words that make up the word *grapevine*? How do they help you understand the whole word *grapevine*? What other words made up of two smaller words can you find in the text?
nosedive	Why do you think a nosedive is called that?

excuse	What are the sounds in the word *excuse* when it is used in the phrase *excuse me*? What does the word *excuse* mean in this phrase? How else can you say the word *excuse*? How does this change the meaning of the word?

MOVING BEYOND THE TEXT

1. What do people use flags for?
2. If you made a flag for yourself, what design would you put on it?
3. Have you ever mistaken one thing for something else? What happened?
4. When have you been brave?

TIME TO WRITE

Write about your favourite kind of race. Would you prefer to be in a running race, a swimming race, a bike-riding race or some other kind of race?